PUFFIN BOOKS

FREE

The U

GW01417981

Another book by Nigel Robinson

Free Willy: The World of Killer Whales

Nigel Robinson

FREE WILLY 2

The Undersea World

Based on the film Free Willy 2
Based on the screenplay written by
Karen Janszen, Corey Blechman *and* John Mattson
Based on characters created by Keith A. Walker

Illustrated by John Butler

PUFFIN BOOKS

PUFFIN BOOKS

Published by the Penguin Group
Penguin Books Ltd, 27 Wrights Lane, London W8 5TZ, England
Penguin Books USA Inc., 375 Hudson Street, New York, New York 10014, USA
Penguin Books Australia Ltd, Ringwood, Victoria, Australia
Penguin Books Canada Ltd, 10 Alcorn Avenue, Toronto, Ontario, Canada M4V 3B2
Penguin Books (NZ) Ltd, 182–190 Wairau Road, Auckland 10, New Zealand

Penguin Books Ltd, Registered Offices: Harmondsworth, Middlesex, England

First published 1995
1 3 5 7 9 10 8 6 4 2

Puffin Film and TV Tie-in edition first published 1995

Typeset by Datix International Limited, Bungay, Suffolk
Filmset in 14/16pt Monophoto Times
Printed in England by Clays Ltd, St Ives plc

Contents

Introduction:
The Tide of Destruction

It's a hot summer's day, and the waves are gently lapping the coastline, filling the tiny rockpools in which countless small animals swim and feed. You're lying on the beach, after clearing a space for yourself among the discarded empty soft-drinks cans and hamburger cartons. You try to ignore the loud music coming from the radio belonging to a group of people down the beach.

In the sky the seagulls are wheeling and squawking so loudly that they're almost drowning out the music. You sit up and watch them skip and glide over the waves, seemingly without a care in the world.

A little way off there's a tiny rocky

promontory: you're really lucky and spot a colony of seals, basking in the warm rays of the sun. They slink off the rocks and dive underwater, where they will probably stay for up to twenty minutes.

Look! Just over there, well beyond the promontory, where the bay widens out into the open sea: an explosion of foam and water, a lightning flash of black. What is it? You shade your eyes from the sun, and gaze out towards the wide ocean. There it is again! Another streak of black, and another, and another, moving very fast. A thrill rushes through you as you recognize the streamlined black bodies, their dorsal fins standing straight and the tell-tale white patches under the eyes.

Orcas! Killer whales! Perhaps as many as twenty, a whole pod, or family, darting and diving through the water with the grace of top ballet dancers and the agility of world-class gymnasts. Perfect harmony, perfect joy: it's one of the most awe-inspiring sights in the animal kingdom.

You try to resist the urge to race out into the sea and join them. They say that orcas, like their dolphin-cousins, are among the

most intelligent creatures on the planet, and you've heard stories of people riding with them before, hitching a ride on their mighty backs. You know that they have a particular affinity with mankind: after all, despite their fish-like appearance, they're mammals, just like us. There are even some people who say that they are just as intelligent as we are.

No, you decide to leave them alone. They're enjoying themselves, romping in the water with their brothers and sisters. It must be great fun, having the entire ocean to play in. For a moment you feel sad for those killer whales that you've seen in marine theme-parks and aquaria, living in small tanks or pens, being forced to perform tricks for human spectators and denied the freedom of the boundless seas.

But at least things are getting better, you recall. More and more people are coming round to the view that it's wrong to keep killer whales – or, indeed, any animals – caged up, when they should be allowed to roam free in their natural habitat, whether it's the seven seas, the plains of Africa, or the rainforests of Brazil. After all, how would you like to be cooped up in a water tank only twenty metres long, performing tricks eight times a day for tourists?

It's only in the oceans of the world that orcas like Willy, Kwatsi and Midnight will be happy and safe, free from man's exploitation of them.

Or will they? There's a strange new smell in the air, mingling uncomfortably with the tangy salt-taste of the sea. It's a dark and bitter smell, and it reminds you of something. You think back to those times when you were travelling with your dad in his car, and he stopped at the local garage to top up the engine with petrol or oil. That's it: oil! But where is it coming from?

There's a new sound in the air now, the sound of helicopters flying in across the sea towards the land. They're spraying something on the water. Something serious is happening, and you peer out into the ocean.

And it's then that you catch sight of it. At first, you see tiny patches of dark on the crests of the waves, as inky-black as the killer whales you've just been watching. And then, as it comes closer, you see that it is a glistening sheet of blackness, a thick, impenetrable film of sludge and ooze: a poisonous blanket of oil covering the sea as far as the eye can see. It's coming towards you now, brought in on the afternoon's high tide, like some implacable monster out of a science-fiction movie.

And then you notice other things in the water, too: seabirds being washed up on the beach, more dead than alive, their wings covered in a coating of oil so heavy that they cannot fly away; depending where you are, you might also catch sight of seals or sea-otters on the rocks, weak and in agony, retching and coughing as they try to rid themselves of the oil that has seeped into

their lungs, clogging their nostrils and making it hard for them to breathe.

The oil has reached the beach now, filling the rocky pools just as the seawater did earlier. You know that the tiny animals living in those pools don't stand a chance. You wonder about the orcas you spotted swimming off the coast, and you pray that at least they may survive.

Like ink on a piece of blotting-paper, the oil sinks into the sand, turning it a horrible, sickening shade of black. You want to throw up, as the cloying stench of the oil reaches your nostrils.

All around you there is death, brought in

on the afternoon tide. Birds and small mammals choke their last, their systems unable to cope with the oil as it oozes into their nostrils, through their mouths and into their lungs. The noisy music fans down the beach are crying now: even they have never seen so much devastation before.

Now the scent of death hangs heavy over the beach, along with the litter and the rubbish. You know that this beach will stay empty for months maybe years, before it is fit to be used again.

It seems foolhardy now to believe, as you did only a short while ago, that Willy and his family, and all the inhabitants of his undersea world, would be safe in the oceans.

One species, among all the millions on this planet, is putting the world and its wildlife at risk. Not just with the oil which comes in on the tide like a Horseman of the Apocalypse, spreading death and devastation. But also with the toxic wastes that are pumped daily into streams and rivers in all the countries of the world, the destruction of the rainforests in South America and the needless hunting of animals.

That species is Man. And if he doesn't come to his senses soon and realize that our planet, Earth, is meant to be shared with all the other living creatures, then he could destroy not only Willy and his fellow whales but perhaps the entire planet.

1

Water, Water Everywhere

Over 70 per cent of the Earth's surface is covered with water – which makes it strange that we should call our home planet the 'Earth'. The largest ocean in the world is the Pacific, which accounts for almost half of the world's seawater: you could quite easily fit a land-mass the size of Europe, Asia and Africa combined into it! It's also been estimated that there's 1,400 million tons of seawater for every person alive today! Over 97 per cent of all the water in the world is to be found in its oceans and seas.

The undersea world is teeming with life. Millions upon millions of fishes swim in its icy depths, where temperatures are so low that no man would survive, and the pressure is so high that a human diver would be crushed to a pulp.

Sea-plants, often a valuable source of food, sway back and forth near the ocean's surface, where there is most sunlight. Scaly creatures, like something out of a horror film, crawl along the sea-bed, ten kilometres down; they are all blind, because no light from the sun ever reaches that far down. Other fish have their own built-in lamps to guide them on their way – batches of fluorescent bacteria which are carried in pouches in their cheeks.

For a place so full of living creatures it's hardly surprising, then, that all life on Earth as we know it – from the tiniest worm to you and me – first started in the sea. About 3,500 million years ago, microscopic-sized bacteria and algae formed in the ocean, feeding off the rich chemical nutrients which floated freely in the water and converting the light from the sun into living tissue.

From this plankton – which still accounts for 90 per cent of all life in the oceans – developed zoo-plankton, equally tiny,

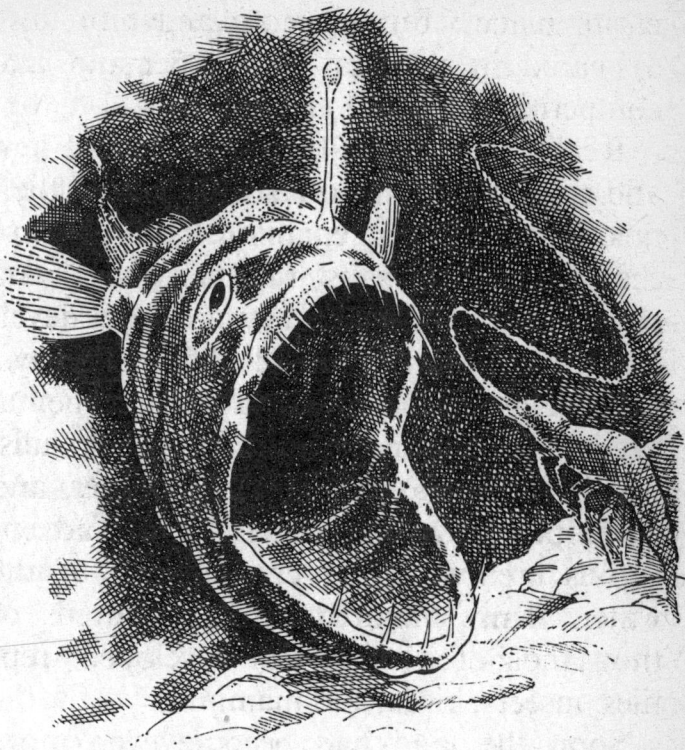

single-celled animals, which fed off the plankton. As millions of years passed, so these minuscule creatures developed, becoming ever more complex, until the first fishes appeared.

For many years the fishes were the Lords of the Deep, which meant that, as there was no life on land, they were the masters of the entire planet. But as more and more fish appeared in the sea so the demand and competition for food grew.

Realizing that the dry land offered a new and rich source of food, some fish lost their fins and grew legs, enabling them to leave the crowded oceans of the world and colonize the land. These new creatures developed in even more and different ways, according to their special environmental needs; for instance, they lost their gills, which fish use to breathe in the water, and developed lungs. And from the first adventurous creatures that crawled out of the water, many hundreds upon hundreds of thousands of new species developed: reptiles, insects, birds, and mammals.

Soon the land had become even more crowded than the oceans had ever been, and competition for food was just as intense. So, about fifty million years ago, one particular land mammal decided to return to the water.

As the years passed, so its body changed once more, adapting itself for a life which would once again be spent entirely in the ocean. Its limbs disappeared and in their place flippers and a strong tail developed, to enable it to move about much more easily in the water and take advantage of the abundance of rich food to be found in the shallow waters around the coast where few mammals went.

It lost most if not all of its body hair, which would slow it down when it was hunting for food; and it streamlined its body so successfully that, even though it was still a mammal, breathing through lungs rather than gills and producing live offspring, it looked much more like a fish. This new creature was the first whale, the ancestor of Willy and his fellow orcas, as well as of dolphins, porpoises and the larger whales.

Other creatures have followed the whales' example and returned to the oceans – penguins and turtles, seals and walruses, for example, spend much of their time in or near the water – but none has been as efficient as the whales in adapting to the different environment. Willy and his friends might just possibly be one of the most successful examples of evolution there has ever been.

*

Willy, Kwatsi and Midnight belong to an order of mammals called cetaceans; this order includes not just killer whales (or orcas) but also dolphins and the much larger whales, such as the sperm whale and the blue whale which, at thirty metres long, is the largest animal ever to have lived on this planet, much larger even than the dinosaurs. A full-grown blue whale can weigh up to 170 tonnes, and just its tongue is equal to the weight of a full-grown elephant!

Cetaceans are divided into two further

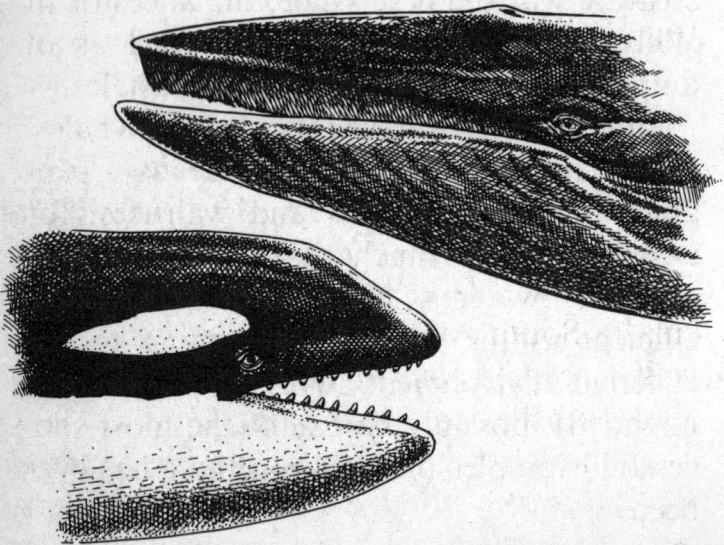

classes: baleen whales, such as the great blue whale, who don't have teeth; and the toothed whales, like Willy, whose forty or so razor-sharp fangs come in handy when they're out hunting the fish that provide them with their staple diet.

Recognizable by the tell-tale white markings on their black bodies and by their huge dorsal fin which can rise two metres above the surface of the water, killer whales like Willy, Kwatsi and Midnight can be seen anywhere in the world. They thrive in all the oceans of the world, from the freezing waters of the Arctic to the more temperate parts of the Caribbean.

However, although they have been spotted in the remotest parts of the oceans, they prefer coastal areas: you're much more likely to see a group of killer whales in shallow waters, like those off the coast of Vancouver Island in Canada or of Patagonia in South America. If you're lucky, you might even catch sight of Willy's fellow orcas off the coast of Britain.

Although whale-spotters may be grateful for the orcas' fondness for coastal waters, this preference can also prove the killer whales' downfall: coastal waters are much more susceptible than the open seas to pollution, especially discharges from oil-tankers, which constantly run the risk of breaking up on the rocks which line our coasts.

However, no matter where you are, it would be extremely unusual if you saw just one killer whale. It's much more likely that you'll see twenty, thirty or even fifty, for orcas are among the most sociable creatures in the entire animal kingdom. They always stay close to their family, or 'pod', which can comprise up to fifty other whales. There are usually more females than males in an orca pod, and orca society is very matriarchal, possibly because the females live to a much greater age than the males.

Each of these pods is made up of several sub-pods, consisting of very close relations, such as brothers and sisters, mother and calves, who will stay together for the whole of their lives, often never venturing more than a couple of hundred metres away from each other. Occasionally these sub-pods may break away from the main pod and go off on their own, but they always return eventually.

In fact, the only thing which can separate a killer whale like Willy from his pod is death – or his capture by humans. Willy and Kwatsi, for instance, were members of a sub-pod, and could hardly bear to be parted from each other.

Jesse realized this when he released Willy in the first *Free Willy* movie; deprived of the company of his fellows, Willy had grown homesick and listless. This is why it's so cruel to keep orcas trapped in pens in marine theme-parks and aquaria: an orca needs the companionship of other orcas, just as you need your friends and relatives around you.

As well as being the most social of animals, orcas also show a remarkable degree

of loyalty to one another. It's not uncommon to see two members of a pod tending to a third, sick, orca by sandwiching it between them to help it stay afloat. And even when one of them is attacked by human hunters or gets caught up in a net, its fellow orcas are reluctant to leave it to its fate and will hang around, showing obvious concern for its well-being. Such selflessness can be their downfall, of course, making it all the more easy for humans to capture and exploit them.

As we shall see later, orcas and their fellow-whales, as well as many of the mammals such as seals and walruses which swim alongside them in the oceans, have suffered greatly at the hand of man – whether being captured in order to become a performing exhibit in a marine theme-park or as a victim of his pollution – so it's amazing to witness the degree of trust which can exist between orcas and human beings. Willy befriended Jesse, but other orcas have been known to save men from drowning, and even to help them in their fishing by herding fish into nets, like dogs directing sheep into a pen!

2

Beach Life

Even though we have scaled the highest mountains and have launched ourselves into space, human beings have always felt a strange affinity for the sea. Even today, about three billion people – that's sixty per cent of the world's population – live within a 100 kilometres of a sea coast. By the year 2000, the United Nations estimates, that number will have increased considerably as the world population reaches six billion.

The seas are very important to us. Before the invention of air travel earlier this century, it was only by sailing across the oceans that we could journey to other countries. Even today many international companies find it much more convenient, and cheaper, to transport valuable cargoes by sea rather than by air-freight. As we shall see, such a method of transportation presents some very real dangers to the creatures who make the seas their home.

Most of us have taken a holiday by the seaside at one time or another, and the thousands of tourists who travel to beach resorts every year provide a valuable source of income for the local residents. Without this income, many of them would go hungry.

Most importantly of all, the seas provide us with much of our food, in the form of fish. Almost all the fish we eat comes from coastal waters, rather than from the deep sea: it's ironic – and more than a little stupid – that our coastal areas are some of the most vulnerable and abused places on our planet.

However, to talk of the seas – in the plural – is as wrong as to call our world the Earth. There is really only one sea, one huge ocean of salt water that covers our entire planet and laps all our shores.

Just as all rivers eventually flow into the

sea, so the Atlantic Ocean flows into the Pacific Ocean, which flows into the Indian Ocean, and, indeed, all the seas in between; there are no natural boundaries between the oceans, as there are on land, where a range of mountains – or even a sea! – may cut off one country from another. The message in that bottle which you throw into the North Sea off the coast of England may eventually be found and read by a Californian living on the shores of the Pacific Ocean.

Even seemingly self-contained 'inland' seas, such as the Mediterranean (until

recently one of the most polluted seas in the world), are connected to the rest of the great World Sea by straits and channels, in this case the Straits of Gibraltar. Throw your bottle – or dump a toxic load of industrial waste – into the Mediterranean and you can never tell where it may end up. It has recently been estimated that a third of all the litter on Scottish beaches does not come from Scotland, but has drifted across the sea from the east coasts of Canada and the USA!

Just as all the seas are dependent on all the other seas, so every single form of life is dependent on every other form of life. From the smallest micro-organisms to Willy's cousins, the mighty blue whales, we are all bound to each other by a complex chain of relationships. In fact, it's not an exaggeration to say that, if you harm one animal, you harm every other animal in that chain.

Let's look at a simple example, not in the sea but on dry land. Imagine that some disaster befell a tiny part of the plains of Africa, so that no more grass grew in that part of the bush. (This isn't quite as far-fetched as it may sound: as cities grow bigger and bigger, so more and more grass-land is being reclaimed for building and industry.) At first you'd think that the lions which roam the plains wouldn't have much cause to worry: after all, they're meat-eaters, and grass plays no part in their diet.

However, the zebra and the gazelle, which the lions feed on, do live on grass and vegetation; with no more grass, they would quickly die out. And, with no more meat to hunt and eat, the lions would soon become extinct as well. Although he's a meat-eater, the lion is dependent on the grass just as much as the zebra: they're linked together in a simple food-chain.

Closer to home, the pesticides with which we spray our fields can also affect the delicate balance of nature. They may be successful in killing off the pests which eat our crops; but what will happen to the cow who, by chance, eats the sprayed crops? And what's going to happen to you or me when we eat our Sunday roast?

As we shall see, even the oceans are not immune. In 1988 a young dolphin was found, dead, off the coast of Wales. In the creature's body were found huge concentrations of chemical compounds, including DDT (which is banned in Britain). None of these chemicals existed naturally, so the dolphin's death was proof of just how much human beings have polluted both the seas and the animals which live in it.

When our oil-tankers spill their cargo into the sea – either deliberately or by accident – the whole balance of nature in the sea can be affected. The oil can harm and even kill off plankton and krill, the microscopic forms of animal and plant life which provide a valuable food-source for many larger animals.

Willy and his family aren't dependent on plankton, and their main diet consists of

fish, seals and penguins. However, their larger cousins, the baleen, or toothless, whales, very much depend on these microscopic creatures. Baleen is the horny, elastic material which hangs down in the mouths of these whales and through which they filter the valuable, nutritious plankton. If the stocks of plankton in the sea are reduced, then these whales have no choice but to go hungry. And even Willy and his fellow orcas aren't immune, as many of the creatures they prey on are dependent on this valuable food-source.

The famous oceanographer, Jacques Cousteau, has even claimed that the pollution of the oceans (caused by man, of course) has already permanently damaged the ultra-thin membrane – or 'neuston' – on the surface of the water; this plays an all-important role in stabilizing the food supplies for plankton. In the ocean, plankton form the first link in the complex food-chain which ultimately supports all the creatures of the deep. If plankton go hungry, then they die. And if the plankton die, then marine animals one step up the food-chain will also go hungry.

3

The Dirty Seas

Parts of the world face the terrible prospect of starving to death. And, as is the case with most things affecting the environment, there is absolutely no need for it to happen. Our farmers, in fact, produce more than enough food to feed every man, woman and child on this planet, but still the World Health Organization estimates that about 780 *million* people in developing countries don't have access to enough food to meet their daily needs, and 180 million children suffer from malnutrition which can lead to death.

The situation can only get worse as the world's population threatens to pass the six billion mark by the year 2000 (at present it stands at about five billion – roughly a third of all the people who have ever lived on Planet Earth).

There are many reasons for this state of affairs: greed on the part of food producers, crop blights and, of course, waste by the industrialized nations. But there is somewhere on Earth where the food supplies are virtually inexhaustible, and it's a place which, until now, has hardly been exploited: the sea.

Apart from being a valuable source in solution of almost every element – magnesium, for example, is already obtained commercially from seawater – it's calculated that we could farm over 200 million tonnes of food from the sea every year, while still leaving plenty for those creatures who live in the ocean.

It seems strange and short-sighted, then, for us to dump often poisonous waste into the sea, especially when we are just investigating the possibilities of farming the sea's valuable food-resources.

Regardless of the effect the thoughtless dumping of much of our waste in the sea has on marine life, we're destroying a potentially enormous source of food for ourselves. But then, until recently, mankind has never given much thought to the environmental consequences of our actions; surely, we say to ourselves, the ocean is big enough to cope with the relatively small amount of pollution we put into it? As we shall see, that isn't necessarily the case.

What is it that we dump in the sea when we are treating it like a huge aquatic dustbin? Mainly it is sewage and industrial waste, waste material from houses, or chemical waste from factories. It's estimated that about eleven million tonnes of industrial waste and fifteen million tonnes of sewage (a tonne is 1,000 kilograms, that is, about nine-tenths the weight of an English ton) are dumped every year into the oceans of the world.

Every year in Britain we get rid of about five thousand tonnes of sewage into the North Sea and a further four thousand tonnes into the Irish Sea. Most of this sewage is treated in sewage works, where it's supposed to be made clean enough to be discharged into the ocean.

However, anyone who has walked along a beach near an industrial town may be forgiven for not believing that: in a recent survey it has been shown that Britain has some of the dirtiest beaches in Europe, and warning notices advising people not to eat any shellfish they may find on the beach are becoming an ever more familiar sight.

Nevertheless, most treated domestic sewage which is pumped out into the sea isn't particularly harmful to marine life. In fact, you'll find that vegetable and plant life is often unusually rich near the mouths of sewers, and most sewage will pass harmlessly into the waters.

But even this isn't without its risks. An excessive pumping of waste into the sea can stimulate the growth of some algae. Algae form a group of plants, of which seaweeds are probably the best known. Now at first sight you might think that this is desirable, until you realize that these algae need oxygen just as much as you or I do.

The presence of more algae can mean that there is less oxygen in the seawater for other species, turning the immediate area into a 'dead zone'. There's one such zone in the Gulf of Mexico, near the mouth of the mighty Mississippi River: this zone is 4,000 square kilometres in size (that's an area bigger than the whole island of Majorca!).

Of more serious concern is the waste which is discharged into the oceans by factories and large industrial complexes. Most of this, too, should be processed through a sewage plant, but there are instances when unscrupulous industrialists have pumped their waste directly into the sea; when they are caught doing this, they can be fined huge sums of money.

However, over 300 million gallons of raw or virtually untreated sewage are discharged into the waters around the British coastline

every day; astonishingly enough, much of this is legal! Here in Britain, the National Rivers Authority issues certain industrial companies with permits to discharge some toxic substances into our rivers up to specified levels: in effect, licences to pollute. However, companies regularly breach these licences and deposit more waste into the rivers than they are allowed to. This is a criminal offence, but prosecutions for such offences are very rare: as low as one per cent. Some of these wastes are highly toxic, for example mercury and cyanide, both of which are poisonous. Even seemingly innocent substances can be deadly: lead absorbed into the system can harm a child's mental development, for instance.

These chemicals are pumped into the water that you bathe in at the seaside, and the viruses and bacteria in it can cause all manner of illnesses, such as vomiting, sore throat and stomach upsets. There is a European standard on the safety on bathing beaches: 23 per cent of British beaches have failed to meet that standard.

Even when these toxic wastes are in a very low concentration (and, to be fair, the proportion of poisonous waste pumped into the sea in relation to the amount of seawater is relatively low), they can still be absorbed by many marine animals, such as fish or mussels, which may suffer no apparent ill-effects. However, many of these waste products can be passed on to us when we eat the fish or seafood that has been caught in the sea and, in the more serious cases, can cause, or aggravate, deadly diseases such as cancer. It's frightening to think that, out of the 70,000 chemicals in industrial use today, one-half are potentially dangerous to human beings.

The effects can be disastrous. Orcas and other marine mammals can take in the pollutants in the water and absorb them into their fatty layers of blubber, or into the milk with which they suckle their young. Poisonous chemical compounds have been found in the bodies of whales, seals and Antarctic penguins, thousands of kilometres away from the source of the pollution! Otters in East Anglia have become so poisoned by chemicals in the rivers that their ability to breed has been harmed.

Humans are at risk, too. Fish caught in

the Irish Sea for human consumption have been found to be contaminated with mercury, and, between 1953 and 1960, hundreds of Japanese living on the shores of Minimita Bay died through eating fish and shellfish which had been contaminated by mercury from industrial effluent.

More frightening still is the amount of radioactive waste that has been dumped into the sea. Nowadays, most of our nuclear waste is disposed of many kilometres underground; but from 1967 until 1982, when the practice was halted, 94,000 tonnes of nuclear waste were dumped in the Atlantic Ocean.

Nuclear waste is encased in supposedly secure containers; but in seas where the pressure can be many thousands of kilograms per square metre, who knows whether these containers have cracked and broken? Who can tell what has happened to that waste now? Who knows whether or not it has filtered throughout the oceans of the world? All we know is that the effects of radioactivity can be terrible on man and animals alike; unlike some chemicals, which can disperse relatively quickly, radioactive isotopes stay active and deadly for centuries,

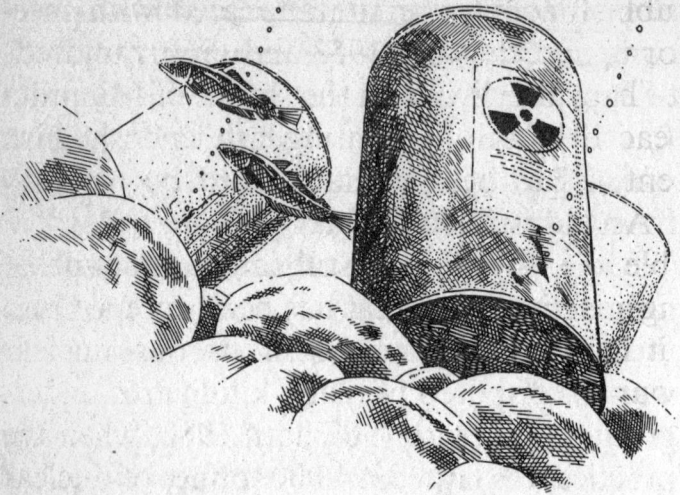

with the potential to harm not just ourselves but also our children and our children's children.

Nor should we forget the pollution that we ourselves cause, as thoughtless individuals. It's estimated that about six and a half tonnes of litter – from soft-drinks cans to hamburger cartons – are left on our beaches every year. A lot of this litter is biodegradable, which means that it eventually decomposes and gets absorbed into the sand – although this is hardly an excuse not to put it in a litter bin! – but more and more of the rubbish we drop on our beaches can survive for up to fifty years, or even longer! In fact, it has been calculated that, along the beaches of the Mediterranean, up to 70 per cent of the litter consists of plastic!

As a single individual you may not be able to stop multinational companies polluting our seas, but you can start to do your bit in cleaning up our planet by taking all your litter home with you!

4

The Black Death

As Jesse and Willy found out to their cost, one of the biggest environmental threats to our beaches and coastline is crude oil. Because oil floats on the surface of the water, its effects are not so noticeable in the open ocean, where most marine animals live far beneath the waves.

But a spillage of crude oil in shallow waters, near the coastline, as happens in *Free Willy 2*, can have terrible and devastating effects on the animals, such as seabirds, seals and orcas, which live near the coast, effects which can linger on for months or even years after the initial accident.

*

Crude oil, or petroleum, is a mineral oil which occurs naturally in nature; it has been known to man since at least the thirteenth century, and probably much earlier than that. It's derived from the remains of countless millions of dead bodies of sea animals and sea plants, which over millions of years have decomposed into the ground to form petroleum.

Oil is essential for many things which we take for granted: we use it for heating, for lubrication, and even in the manufacture of plastics. Although its first modern use was as a replacement for whale oil in lamps, petroleum really came into its own with the invention of the motor car. Nowadays life would be unthinkable without this 'black gold' which comes out of the earth.

This oil seeps out naturally from the earth both on the ground and at sea level, with few if any consequences for marine life. However, it's when a massive amount of crude oil is discharged into the ocean over a short period of time – when an oil-tanker runs aground, for instance – that all hell can break loose and thousands upon thousands of animals can be killed and the delicate balance of nature destroyed, sometimes for ever.

Of all the causes of oil pollution in the mid-1980s, it's estimated that only 8 per cent were from natural seepages into the oceans. The rest were all down to man's carelessness and his unthinking attitude to the world and the oceans around him.

Crude oil is big business; every day, thousands of oil-tankers carry their valuable cargo along the waterways of the world. It's not surprising, then, that tankers are ultimately responsible for almost half of the crude oil which pollutes our seas, with about a third coming from municipal and industrial waste discharges.

Contrary to popular belief, oil spills from wrecked tankers don't seem to be the biggest cause of crude-oil pollution. Only about 12 per cent of the oil poisoning our seas comes from tankers running aground and spilling their load.

The United Nations estimates that an amazing 21 per cent is down to tankers discharging part of their load either accidentally or as a routine matter of course, in order to empty their tanks of unwanted oil!

That's about one million tonnes of the 1.6 million tonnes discharged annually by ships! Accidental maritime oil-spills happen on average about three times a day.

However, because most oil-tanker accidents occur in coastal waters, the consequences are longer-lasting and much more severe. There are still huge globules of oil floating in the world's oceans from tanker spillages of years ago; in the Mediterranean it wasn't an uncommon event for fishermen to pull up their nets to find that their nets were full, not of fish, but of huge balls of tar! However, between 1976 and 1986 there has been a sizeable reduction in oil-spills, largely due to a 25 per cent drop in the amount of oil carried by sea, but thanks also to a series of international regulations regarding safety.

Almost all the world's oil companies have shown some good sense and have signed voluntary agreements to pay for whatever damage they may cause to the seas and marine life in the event of an oil-spill. This still doesn't prevent dishonest and unprincipled operators – like the villains in the movie – sailing under 'flags of convenience'. By sailing with the flag of certain countries, such as Liberia, they try to avoid some international safety and environmental regulations, as well as evading corporate responsibility for any oil-spillages they may cause.

The consequences of an oil-spillage from a tanker, or an oil blow-out from an off-shore oil-drilling operation, can be enormous. For example, when the tanker the *Amoco Cadiz* ran aground off the coast of Brittany in northern France, way back in 1978, it caused massive pollution. It spilled 200,000

tonnes of crude oil into the sea, killing off 30,000 seabirds, as well as about 230,000 tonnes of fish and shellfish, along 150 kilometres of Britanny's coastline. Ten years later, France was awarded over $85 million as compensation: such a sum was hardly enough to cover the cost of cleaning up the oil-spillage, and the damage to marine life and the environment had been incalculable.

In 1974, the tanker *Metula* spilt 47,000 tonnes of crude oil on the beaches of Tierra del Fuego, at the southernmost tip of Argentina. The main species affected by this disaster were cormorants, 2,000 of which were killed almost immediately, a further 2,000 dying slow and lingering deaths later. Their coats covered with oil which clogged their eyes and choked them, dead cormorants were found up to a kilometre inland. Mussels and other shellfish were also affected, making them unfit for human consumption.

Such accidents also happen much nearer to home. Ask anybody over the age of thirty who lived on or near the coast of Cornwall at the time, and they'll still remember with dread the night of 16 March 1967, when the *Torrey Canyon* ran aground, only twenty-five kilometres west of Land's End. The supertanker was carrying 119,000 tonnes of crude oil in its hold when its sides were pierced by the treacherous rocks found along that part of the coastline. About 100,000 tonnes of crude oil were released into the sea; the only reason why the remaining oil wasn't allowed to spill into the sea was because emergency aircraft managed to fly out to the site of the wreck and bomb it, thereby setting the remaining oil on fire and thus minimizing its pollution of the English Channel. The sea itself was ablaze for days.

For five days the oil slick moved inexorably towards the Cornish coast like a remorseless, black tide of death; despite all their efforts, the emergency forces (called in by the Ministry of Defence, for this was as serious as any bloody battle with enemy forces) were powerless to halt its progress; when it finally hit the Cornish beaches, over 30,000 seabirds had been killed, and many seals and other marine animals found themselves in trouble.

But that wasn't the end of the oil-slick from the *Torrey Canyon*. Blown by winds and strong tides, which had hindered the authorities trying to disperse the oil, parts of the slick continued on their relentless advance of death and destruction towards the Channel Islands and, from there, on to the coast of Brittany in France.

Six weeks after the *Torrey Canyon* had first struck the rocks, globules and slicks of oil were still coming ashore on the French coast; the last traces of oil were finally dispersed in early June, almost two months later. The wreck of the *Torrey Canyon* had been a disaster beyond belief and, even today, it ranks as one of the largest marine disasters in the world in terms of its impact on the environment.

Yet even that seems small game when compared to the biggest oil spillage in the world. This came in January 1991, at the height of the Gulf War after Iraq invaded Kuwait, whose economy is almost entirely dependent on its rich reserves of oil. To ensure that his enemies wouldn't be able to get their hands on the Kuwaitis' oil, Iraq's leader, Saddam Hussein, deliberately discharged almost *one and a half million tonnes* of oil into the ocean, creating the biggest oil-slick the world has ever known and causing the deaths of tens of thousands of marine creatures. It was a callous, irresponsible and wanton act of destruction which will affect that part of the world for many years to come.

The largest oil-spill so far in the coastal waters of the United States of America happened on 24 March 1983. The tanker *Exxon Valdez* was sailing through the Prince William Sound, near the coast of Alaska. In its huge tanks it was carrying a quarter of a million barrels of oil – that's about 45 million litres.

The twenty-fourth of March was a dark and cold night, a night of high winds and rough seas. Suddenly the tanker lurched sideways and there was a sickening *crunch!* Whether by accident or by human error, the tanker had foundered on a rock, the razor-sharp sides of which sliced into the hull of the ship as effortlessly as a hot knife cuts through butter. Oil began to pour out of its tanks like blood being pumped out through an open wound, until 37,000 tonnes of thick, viscous crude had turned the clear Arctic waters into black, foul-smelling sludge.

An emergency call goes out, but the rescue services are slow to respond. The winds are too high and the seas too storm-tossed, and already the slick is spreading out. As each minute passes, it becomes even more difficult to contain. Within two weeks it will have travelled 250 kilometres away from the tanker (roughly equivalent to the distance between London and Manchester) and will have covered an area of 4,000 square kilometres. Some 11,000 square kilometres of Alaskan shoreline will have been affected, and most of the sea-otters in the area, as well as at least 36,000 seabirds, will have died.

A massive dispersal operation – which will cost the company owning the *Exxon Valdez* a million dollars a day – will be able to do little to clean up the area; even now, six years after the disaster, this part of Alaska still remains extremely polluted, a sobering testimony to man's ability to foul his own environment.

It has been estimated that the oil from the *Exxon Valdez* killed more wildlife than any other oil-spill in history. As well as the seabirds which lost their lives, the seal population in the area was reduced by over a third. Examination of dead seals revealed that they had suffered the sort of brain damage that is also found in humans who have died from glue-sniffing and solvent abuse. Nor were the orcas immune either. A pod of orcas which lived in the Sound lost seven of its members, and six more members disappeared the following year.

Fish are relatively immune to pollution from all but the biggest oil-slicks. However, when the *Braer* oil-tanker was wrecked off the Shetland Islands in 1993, many thousands of fish did die, including inshore and deep-water species. Four days after the *Braer* was grounded, the government closed some local fishing grounds, fearing that the fish caught there would be poisonous to humans. Shetland farmers reported that two-and-a-half million salmon had been affected by the oil-spillage, effectively ruining an entire crop of fish.

As we have seen, it is the smaller marine animals, especially mammals such as orcas, seals and otters, which suffer most from the oil spilled from tankers. The smaller creatures are smothered by the sticky dark crude, and die through lack of food or light; others, such as Willy, Kwatsi and Midnight, are poisoned, or find it difficult to breathe as the crude seeps into their nostrils and lungs.

Remember: even though orcas look like giant fish, they're mammals, just like you and me; as such, they breathe through their lungs, not through gills as fish do. Like any human diver, from time to time they must come up to the surface of the ocean to breathe; in fact, one of the commonest causes of death among whales and dolphins is drowning!

When Midnight and Kwatsi were rescued from the oil-spill, they were both close to death because the crude spilled from the *Largo* was incredibly toxic (that is, poisonous) to their lungs and internal organs. Their blowhole, the tiny hole on the top of their 'head', was also blocked by the gunge, making it difficult for them to breathe.

A whale's blowhole acts as its nostrils through which it breathes; it is to be found on the top of its head (rather than at the front of its 'face', as our nostrils are) for one very good reason: it's this part which breaks through the water first when the whale rises to the surface to breathe.

When the whale rises to the surface, it expels a lot of used air – just as a human diver would after swimming underwater – before breathing in fresh air. This action is probably what has given rise to the myth that whales and dolphins expel *water* through their blowholes: when the expelled warm air comes into contact with the cooler surrounding air, it turns to water vapour, which to any passing sailor would look very

much like a fountain of water shooting out of the whale's blowhole.

When Kwatsi and Midnight rose from the depths then, the first thing they would have breathed in would have been the crude from the oil-slick. Imagine how you would feel if you had no choice but to inhale crude oil that some tanker had belched out into the ocean!

As an oil-slick moves along on the surface of the sea, some of the oil does evaporate, but most of it is stirred and whipped up by the waves and wind into a dark-brown emulsion, or oil-in-water solution. Scientists call this substance 'chocolate mousse', because that's exactly what it looks like! This chocolate mousse is extremely difficult to remove but, depending on the circumstances, there are several ways in which one can attempt to disperse it.

One of the most common ways is to remove it with emulsifiers or detergents. However, while these detergents certainly do help to disperse the deadly mousse, many marine animals are allergic to the chemicals in the detergent, and so this method can often cause just as many problems as it solves!

When the *Torrey Canyon* spilt its load, much of the resultant oil-spillage was treated with detergent. However, while this method helped to clear up the oil, it also dissolved in the water and caused the deaths of many off-shore creatures, including crabs and lobsters. Detergents are used sparingly now, as we come to realize just how much we are harming marine life.

To clear up the *Torrey Canyon* spillage, as we saw, the Royal Navy set fire to some of the oil, so that it would burn itself off before it could do any further damage to sea life. This can be a highly effective way of getting rid of the crude, but it requires a speedy response from the rescue services; they must reach the oil before it absorbs too much seawater, otherwise they'll be unable to set it ablaze. Some 20,000 tonnes of crude oil were disposed of in this way in the *Torrey Canyon* disaster; but 100,000 tonnes remained to pollute the south-western coast of England for months to come.

A major problem with spilt oil is that it floats on the surface and doesn't sink. If it did, it would be absorbed and diluted into

the seawater over such a great area that it would be rendered relatively harmless. Very often, fine powder, or even sand or gravel, is dropped on to an oil-slick in an effort to 'sink' it. This is how the French navy successfully got rid of the last of the oil slicks threatening the Brittany coast in the aftermath of the *Torrey Canyon* disaster.

In efforts to render oil-slicks as safe as possible, use has even been made of 'scavenging' materials such as hay or straw, which absorb the oil but stay floating on the surface of the water, making it easier for recovery ships to scoop up all the oil.

5

Candles, Soap and Corsets

In *Free Willy 2* we have seen how man destroys his environment through greed, ignorance or selfishness, threatening not only his own future but also the well-being and survival of the other creatures with whom he shares this planet.

'But it's our planet, isn't it?' some people say. 'Don't we have a right to do what we want with it?' We human beings have a tendency to think that we're the most important animals on the planet (and, after all, that's all we really are: animals), without realizing that we're just a small part of one huge ecological system.

In reality, mankind is a relative newcomer, our species, *Homo sapiens*, having been around for only a little under 40,000 years. Willy and his kind have been ruling the waves for a considerably longer time – fifty million years more, in fact. And if a mysterious plague suddenly wiped mankind out overnight, most other creatures would happily go on living without us: in fact, they'd probably thrive. Man's sudden extinction, for instance, would pose no problem for the millions of different species of insects – except for the three breeds of lice which live off human beings! So much for us having a special right to regard this planet as our own!

In fact, many other animals seem to be just as intelligent as we are – if not more so. Willy and his fellow orcas, for instance, have highly developed social structures, staying in the same family, or 'pod', all their lives – unless, that is, they are captured by man and taken from the family to a marine theme-park, to perform there like a circus clown for our 'amusement'.

They show an amazing degree of co-operation, too, when hunting for food. In the frozen wastes of the Antarctic, where human beings cannot venture without special protection, killer whales swim freely. Seals form the main part of their diet there, and it's certainly not uncommon for two orcas to swim underneath an ice-floe on which a seal is resting, and tilt it up so that the seal slides off the floe – straight into the jaws of a waiting third orca! Such careful pre-planning is worthy of a crack SAS team, and is surely proof of the orcas' intelligence.

No one knows for sure just how many different species of life exist on Planet Earth today. Some people estimate that there could be as many as eighty million species; others think that there are as few as five million different varieties of mammals, reptiles, insects, fishes and plants. Certainly only about one and a half million have so far been described and catalogued – although more are being discovered and identified every year – and there may be many, many others about which we will never know, especially in the deeps of the ocean where no man has ever been.

The sea still holds many mysteries, and it is constantly surprising mankind. One of its more recent surprises was the coelacanth, a large, ugly-looking fish which everyone thought had been extinct for many millions of years – until a live one was caught off the coast of Africa in 1930! What other discoveries might the sea yield to us in the future? In fact, we now know more about the Moon, our nearest neighbour in space, than we do about the seas which surround our continents.

We may never know just how many species we share our planet with, but there is one thing of which we can be certain: at least one-quarter of the species living on the Earth today, from the tiniest flower in the Amazonian rainforest to the mightiest blue whale swimming in the oceans of the world, is in danger of becoming extinct in the next twenty to thirty years. And, by the end of this century, up to one million species will have vanished from the surface of the Earth.

Think about that for a moment. Look around your class. Imagine that seven or eight of them could be dead in twelve hours' time. It's a pretty scary thought, isn't it? And that's exactly what's about to happen to the Earth if we don't do something about it.

Extinction of species can, of course, be part of the natural order of things: one species dies and another takes over. The dinosaurs are a good example. We tend to think of them as failures when it comes to survival, but they were the undisputed masters of this planet for 150 million years (remember, the first *Homo sapiens* appeared only about 40,000 years ago!). No one's quite sure why they died out, sixty-five million years ago, although some scientists believe that a huge meteorite struck the Earth, sending up a cloud of dust and rubble so thick that the light of the sun was blocked out for many years, leaving the dinosaurs to starve and freeze to death.

However, mammals with their thick woolly coats were able to survive the change in temperature much better than the dinosaurs and, as time went on, one mammal in particular, a shrewish-looking creature that was constantly hiding from the mighty lizards, rose to particular prominence: mankind. So you could say that, if the dinosaurs hadn't become extinct, we would still be burrowing in holes in the ground!

Over the past 400 years, however, more and more species have been dying out at an even faster rate. In Africa the elephant population is being halved each decade. In 1979 there were 1.3 million elephants roaming the plains of Africa; by 1988 that number was down to 740,000. Approximately 15,000 black rhinos were alive in 1980; five years later, less than half that number remain.

Willy, Kwatsi and their fellow killer whales aren't in any particular danger of becoming extinct, but some of their cousins aren't so lucky. And once again, their predicament is down to mankind's greed and his thoughtless misuse of his environment.

A high proportion of living creatures kill. In the depths of the Atlantic, orcas will kill seals, fish and sometimes even much larger whales; on the great plains of the Serengeti, a pride of lions will mercilessly stalk a zebra or gazelle; in the skies, hawks and eagles will swoop down on small rodents and carry them away to feed to their chicks. There's nothing wrong with this; all these animals are meat-eaters, and they have to kill to survive.

Among all the millions on Planet Earth, there is only one animal that kills, not just to eat, but also for pleasure (they call it 'sport') and for profit. And the name of that animal? That's right: man.

Men have hunted whales since the beginning of time. The first record of whaling we have was found on the walls of prehistoric caves in Norway, and the people who lived by the cold waters of the north were probably the very first whalers.

The modern tradition of whaling seems to have begun about 1100 among the Basque people of southern France and northern Spain. On sighting a whale, they would put out to sea and, using blazing torches, would drive the confused and frightened whale on to the shore. Once the whale was beached, they would cut the defenceless creature up before distributing its meat to members of the community. It has even been suggested that the word 'harpoon' might come from the old Basque word *arpoi*, which means 'to catch alive'.

These Basque sailors caught whales for

their meat and oil. Initially they hunted only in waters close to the coast, but, as the whales became scarcer and scarcer, they ventured further out to sea. Still, although their methods of killing the trapped whale might be regarded as cruel, at least they killed the whale for its meat, just as modern-day farmers may kill a pig for the pork it provides.

In the seventeenth century there was a great development in whaling, with not just the Spanish but north-west Europeans hunting the right whales which live near the coast of Greenland. These whales were called 'right' whales, because when they were killed they conveniently floated on the surface, rather than sinking to the bottom of the sea: they were the 'right' whales to kill.

The right whales were easy prey for the whalers, because they were very slow movers (unlike Willy and the orcas, who are so fast that they can cover 150 kilometres a day in the open sea, although fifty kilometres a day is much more common). The hunting of the right whales made that species almost extinct.

Almost as soon as the settlers arrived on

the east coast of America in the seventeenth century, they also started whaling, hunting not only the right whale but also the humpback; and the Russians started to set up commercial whaling stations at about the same time. Very soon all the maritime countries of the world were mercilessly hunting down Willy's ancestors.

If you wanted to make lots of money, there were few better professions to take up than whaling. One whale could make its killers several thousands of pounds and, as each whaling ship would catch and kill up to seventy whales a year, the profits were enormous. Whaling soon became big business: you'll find an excellent account of whaling in the nineteenth century in the

novel, *Moby Dick*, written by the American author Herman Melville. So successful was this business that, of one million sperm whales, only 10,000 are now left; there are only 4,000 humpback whales left from an original population of 20,000; and less than 1,000 blue whales now swim in the seas where there used to be a quarter of a million.

But what were whales being hunted and killed for? While it's true that some sailors hunted them for their meat, most whalers were interested in more mundane things. The flesh of the sperm whale, for instance, is not particularly tasty; however, its blubber, the insulating layer of fat beneath its skin, was a valuable source of oil used to make candles and soap.

A substance called ambergris is to be found in the large intestine of the same whale. It's a grey, waxy substance, consisting mainly of cholesterol, and it has a distinctive musty odour. The whalers of the eighteenth and nineteenth centuries had no idea why ambergris should be found in the sperm whale's gut – but that hardly mattered to them. What was important to them was that there were hundreds of perfume-makers back home who would pay good money for the ambergris, which they used as a stabilizer in the perfumes they concocted and sold to rich women.

Another valuable by-product from a slaughtered toothless whale, such as the right whale, was its baleen. This horny substance, sometimes called whalebone, was used to strengthen crinolines, and as a stiffener in women's corsets!

Candles, soap, perfumes and corsets: that's what the world's whales were being hunted for.

By the 1800s, stocks of right whales were almost completely wiped out in the chilly waters of the Arctic, but still the killings went on. Man seemed obsessed with hunting down the whales. By 1850 there were more than 700 whaling ships at sea. There was a temporary decline in whaling in the late nineteenth century, but the introduction of speedier and more powerful ships meant that faster-moving whales, such as the rorqual, could now be caught.

The slaughter began again, and it continues right up to the present time. As the number of whales in the northern oceans of the world became severely reduced, so whalers turned their attention to the Antarctic oceans. Today, most of the whales hunted in the seas are killed for their meat; this has always been considered a great culinary delicacy, especially by the Japanese; until recently, however, whale meat was also used as pet food!

It was only in the 1930s that the world finally woke up to the fact that something had to be done, otherwise several species of whales would soon become extinct. Once there were a quarter of a million blue whales in the southern oceans; now there are as few as one thousand. In the 1940s the International Whaling Commission was set up, with the aim of regulating the exploitation of whales. Even with the existence of the Commission, about 70,00 whales were still being annually slaughtered as recently as the 1960s.

In 1986 most of the whaling and non-whaling nations of the world agreed that there should be a ban on commercial whaling. However, despite this ban, 14,000 whales have still been killed since 1986, many by the whalers of Norway and Japan, the latter being the world's biggest consumers of whale meat, which they eat either raw or cooked with ginger.

It's not only whales which are facing bloody slaughter at the hands of man. Willy's close relatives, the dolphins and porpoises, are also at risk. In the ten years between 1982 and 1992, Japan was responsible for the deliberate deaths of 300,000 dolphins and porpoises; even when they aren't being hunted for their meat, many dolphins are killed when they get tangled up in underwater drift-nets which are designed to trap much smaller fish, such as tuna. Even sperm whales can become caught up in these nets of death, whose almost indestructible synthetic fibres can trap and hold a whale as securely as any manacles. Up to 8,000 whales and dolphins a year die in these drift-nets off the Italian coast alone: in 1993 the environmental organization, Greenpeace, found thirteen sperm whales trapped in Italian nets.

6

The Land of the Walrus

Willy and his fellow orcas and dolphins are among the most graceful and intelligent mammals living in the sea. Yet there are many other marine mammals who share the ocean with them – as well as the ever-present threat of death at the hands of men.

Seals, sea-lions and walruses belong to a group of mammals called pinnipedia, which mean fin- or feather-footed; like Willy, their ancestors returned to the sea many millions of years ago, to take advantage of the abundant food supplies there. Unlike Willy, they also live on the land, although they seem just as much at home in the water.

True seals are distinguishable by their

flippers, which are covered by hair on all the surfaces; their hind flippers are stretched back, with their soles opposed, and this makes them very clumsy movers on land when they try to get about in a series of wriggling and sliding movements. However, when they slide into the water they prove themselves to be one of the most graceful mammals in the world.

The hind flippers of sea-lions, on the other hand, can be turned beneath its body so that it can walk on land: the Californian sea-lion, which possesses a great sense of balance and can clap its flippers and balance a ball on its snout, is the creature we most often think of as a sea-lion, and it's usually these creatures one sees at marine theme-parks.

Walruses are the giants of the pinnipedia family, recognizable by their bristly 'moustaches' and their tusks, which can reach a length of a metre. Walruses can grow to four metres in length and weigh up to 1,350 kilograms.

Seals and their cousins are to be found in all the oceans of the world, although they prefer to live in shallow coastal waters

rather than in the open sea. There's even a colony of seals living in Lake Baikal, in Siberia, the sixth largest freshwater lake in the world. They're most common, however, in the Arctic and Antarctic oceans, although it's not unusual to catch sight of a group of seals basking in the sun on the rocks off the British coast.

Willy and the whales have been much more successful in adapting their bodies to enable them to live entirely in the water; but seals must spend at least part of each day on the land. They can, however, dive underwater for up to twenty minutes when required to – no mean achievement, when you consider that a man, without artificial breathing apparatus, can stay underwater for only two to three minutes!

Of course, like all mammals, seals need oxygen to survive; without oxygen, all mammals suffer irreversible brain-damage. Seals manage to survive underwater for such long periods of time by conserving huge amounts of oxygen in their blood and feeding it to their brains. People who have cut open a dead seal are often surprised at the amount of blood which flows out of its carcass – one and three-quarters as much as from a man of similar size and weight: it's this vast supply of blood which enables the seal to spend such long periods underwater.

The seal has also adapted its body in other ways to enable it to survive in its underwater environment. Like Willy, its body is streamlined, with few projections, making it ideally suited for speeding through the water. It also has very large eyes, which are out of all proportion to its face and which allow it to take in as much light as possible, so that it can see in the inky depths of the ocean, as it goes hunting for fish which, together with krill, form the main part of its diet.

Its sense of smell is also good; and it is

believed that it uses a system called 'echo-location' to help it track down its food. Echo-location is a system whereby a mammal emits a series of high-pitched sounds then listens for the echoes, which are reflected off objects ahead of it, to calculate the distance. This is a great way to 'see' in deep waters, and is an ability which is also shared by Willy and the whales.

Again like Willy and his cousins, seals are trusting and very inquisitive – something which can prove their downfall when approached by vicious human hunters – and they are also very social, often grouping together in large colonies on the rocky shores. (Their family set-up isn't quite as close as Willy's, though: there are many seals which are quite happy being by themselves, except during the breeding season.)

While seals are not in as great danger of being driven to extinction as are some of the larger whales, they have still been exploited needlessly and cruelly by man. Perhaps the only people who can claim with some justification to be allowed to hunt seals are the Innuits of the far north. Seals provide the Innuits with much of their meat; indeed, without seal meat, life for them would be impossible. When a seal is killed, the Innuits ensure that every piece of its carcass is used. Just as with the walruses, which are especially prized by the Innuits for their ivory tusks, they eat seal meat, and they also use sealskin to protect themselves from the biting sub-zero temperatures of their homeland; they extract oil from the seal's blubber to fuel their lamps and they use other parts of its body to make rope and tools.

While the Innuits have always respected the seal, other hunters have been less scrupulous, killing literally millions of seals for their furs. Even today the common and ringed seals are still slaughtered for their furs – although thankfully not in such great numbers as years ago, when seals were clubbed to death, rather than shot with a rifle, so that their prized hides weren't spoilt by any unnecessary holes.

Perhaps even more horrific and stomach-turning than the mass slaughter of seals to give their fur to the fashionable is the annual slaughter of thousands of baby seals. Some people call it 'culling'; others call it mass murder.

At the turn of the century, the grey seal was in danger of dying out completely. There were only about 500 left in the entire world, the rest having been hunted to extinction for their valuable furs. A law was then passed, forbidding the hunting of the grey seal during their breeding season, which was the time when they were most vulnerable.

The strategy seemed to work. Within fifteen years, numbers had increased to about 8,000 and were rising. However, complaints soon arose from the local fishermen who worked along the coasts where the seals chose to congregate, lying on the rocks and basking in the sun. The seals were making holes in their fishing nets, the fishermen claimed, ruining the season's catch; or, worse, they were actually eating the fish themselves, thereby depleting the stock of fish in the ocean! (No one, it seems, ever considered the fact that there's more than enough fish in the sea both for fishermen and for seals . . .)

Faced with a choice between the seals' needs and a possible drop in the seamen's income, there seemed to be only one solution: a culling of the seals, to keep their number down. But which seals should they kill? Killing the males – or bulls – would have no effect on the seal population. Bulls are polygamous creatures, having a harem of several different mates; if one bull was killed, another bull would simply move in on his 'widowed' mates and start breeding with her. It was also found to be impractical to kill the females; this left only one alternative.

Baby seals, or pups, some only a few weeks old, are mercilessly killed, to keep the seal population down. It's also easier to dispose of their smaller carcasses; the fact that their pelts are of a high quality and very marketable is an added bonus.

While there are arguments on both sides, for and against the culling of seals, most members of the public seem, at the very least, to be uneasy about this wholesale massacre of baby seals, and cries of protest are invariably heard wherever and whenever it happens. However, even today, Canadian fishermen are asking their government for permission to revive the seal trade, claiming that the seals are eating fish stocks off the Gulf of Saint Lawrence in Newfoundland.

7

Home, Sweet Home?

Planet Earth is all we've got. We can't blast off into outer space to another planet when we grow fed up with this one. So it makes sense to look after it, doesn't it? After all, if you can't be bothered to clean your house or flat, pretty soon germs and diseases are going to breed; even if they don't kill you, they can make your life so miserable that the idea of doing the household chores will seem like the greatest idea in the world. The trouble is, by that time it'll be too late. We don't treat our home like a rubbish tip, so it's time we wised up and stopped treating our universal home – Planet Earth, to you and me – like one.

Thankfully, some people are starting to wake up and take notice of the way we've been mistreating our planet, and they are finally doing something about it. Over both the North and the South Poles we've spotted the holes in the ozone layer, the protective barrier shielding Planet Earth from the sun's harmful ultra-violet rays which can cause cancer. These holes are still getting bigger, but at least we've started to try to do something about them by restricting the use of CFCs (or chlorofluorocarbons), man-made chemicals which are now being used less and less in aerosol cans and refrigerators, since we discovered that they are partially responsible for destroying the ozone layer.

We've realized that, just a few thousand years ago, rainforests were covering about 14 per cent of the Earth – about two billion hectares. Now over half of those forests have been destroyed, most of them in the past 200 years. The trees and plants in these forests 'breathe in' carbon dioxide and 'breathe out' oxygen which all animals on Earth depend on for their survival. Contrary to what many people say, the rainforests aren't the 'lungs of the world', because there are far greater sources of oxygen on Planet Earth; but the fewer rainforests there are, the greater will be the amount of carbon dioxide in the atmosphere. And the more carbon dioxide there is in the air, the more the Earth's temperature will rise, because carbon dioxide traps the sun's heat. And the further the temperature rises, the more the polar ice-caps will melt. And the more the ice-caps melt, then the higher the level of the sea will rise. Is it any wonder that many people who live in low-lying countries like Holland (and parts of England, too) are starting to think twice about chopping down another tree in the Amazon basin? Every little thing we do here on Planet Earth has a consequence for every other living thing on this planet.

And, at long last, we're starting to recognize that we can't continue to foul our own environment, because by doing so we're simply harming ourselves. You don't even have to be noble and self-sacrificing to make a stand against pollution: being totally self-ish works just as well. Remind your dad of this the next time he pours the last of his car's oil down the drain. Ask him where it goes. Into the sewers, of course. And then into the sea, and then probably into a fish which, if he's unlucky, he'll be eating for dinner in a couple of weeks' time. *Now* how does he fancy that meal of cod and chips?

We ought to take a little time to consider the plight of the creatures we share Planet Earth with, many of which have been around for many millions of years longer than ourselves – creatures like Willy's ancestors, which had elaborate social networks and sophisticated communication skills when Neanderthal man, our ancestor, still couldn't quite figure out how to start a fire, or what a wheel was for, let alone how to make one.

International laws have been brought into force, banning – or limiting – the number of whales and/or seals that may be hunted every year. It's not a perfect state of affairs – and some nations (Norway is one) have resumed commercial whaling in spite of vociferous international protests – but at least it's a start. And the selling and transportation of ivory has been made illegal in those countries where the elephant and the rhino-

ceros face danger at the very least and, at the very worst, total extinction.

You'll never see real fur coats on the catwalks of the top fashion shows nowadays, because all the big-name and trendy designers have realized that killing animals simply to pander to human vanity is not only cruel (remember the baby seals) and immoral, it's seriously stupid as well.

We're also getting round to ending sentencing animals to a lifetime's imprisonment in cages at zoos. While animals in many zoos are excellently looked after, still their life behind bars can scarcely compare to their previous existence in the wide-open savannahs or, in Willy's case, in the endless oceans, where he could dine off live fish rather than the frozen dead fish many performing orcas, dolphins and sea-lions are given at marine theme-parks. And who would want to see animals in cages, when they could watch them on TV in the many wildlife programmes, which are, understandably and deservedly, among the most popular shows on television?

You can do *your* bit to help make both the world a cleaner place and the lives of our fellow animals a happier and more secure one, and you'll find a list of useful addresses opposite.

But remember: it's up to you to clean up our one home, and to look after and care for all the other creatures who live on Planet Earth. There's hope for us all, even though it's taken mankind 40,000 years to learn the lesson that Willy's ancestors had learnt fifty million years ago.

We all of us, from the mightiest blue whale to the smallest single-celled amoeba, share the same home.

And it's the only planet we've got.

If you want to find out more about killer whales, or marine pollution, write to one of the following organizations. Please do remember to enclose a stamped self-addressed envelope with your letter if you want a reply.

Whale and Dolphin Conservation
  Society
19A James Street West
Bath
Avon BA1 2BT

World Wide Fund For Nature
Panda House
Weyside Park
Godalming
Surrey GU7 1XR

Friends of the Earth
56–58 Alma Street
Luton LU1 2PH

Greenpeace Ltd
Canonbury Villas
London N1 2PN

RICHIE RICH
A novelization by Todd Strasser

Twelve-year-old Richie Rich has everything money can buy: a billion dollar estate, a private butler, even his own fast-food restaurant! All Richie wants is to fit in with the kids in the neighbourhood. Unfortunately Peewee, Omar, Gloria and Tony just laugh at him. After all, whoever heard of someone playing baseball in a suit?

But when a dishonest employee of Rich Enterprises tries to take over the company, it's up to Richie to save the day. He needs all the help he can get, and Peewee, Gloria and the gang get to see a whole new side of the boy billionaire. Now Richie must find his parents, protect his friends and save the family fortune!

DUMB AND DUMBER
A novelization by Madeline Dorr

Meet Harry Dunne and Lloyd Christmas. Two really dumb guys. No-hopers. In fact, they're practically the biggest goofballs in the history of the world.

They drive a van dressed up to look like a dog. Lloyd's big idea for a successful business is a worm factory and Harry likes licking frost.

But now, they've had enough, they want a change. A new life beckons on the ski slopes of Aspen, Colorado, and what better way to start than by travelling 500 miles in the wrong direction?

BLACK BEAUTY
*A novelization by Catherine R. Daly from the
book by Anna Sewell*

The classic tale of a beautiful black stallion.

In a lantern-lit stable on Farmer Grey's estate a coal-black foal is born. With a gleaming star on his forehead and a matching white sock on his left hind leg, Black Beauty is at first cared for and cherished. But fate deals him a cruel blow and Black Beauty finds himself in the dark and dangerous streets of Victorian London.

This is perhaps one of the best-loved children's stories of all time and has now been made into a stunning film.